14.95

T2-BRN-831

D0566393

I
Really Want
to Dance

RICHARD GLASSTONE
DAVID HODGSON
Photographs by
SIMON RAE-SCOTT

I Really Want to Dance

THAMES/METHUEN

Acknowledgments

The authors wish to thank the Director of
the Royal Ballet School, Mr James
Monahan, the school's Ballet Principal,
Miss Barbara Fewster and the Headmistress of
White Lodge, Mrs Helen Kastrati, as well
as Mr Nicholas Jones of Thames
Television International Ltd for
making the publication of this book
possible.

British Library Cataloguing in Publication Data

Glasstone, Richard
    I really want to dance.
    1. Royal Ballet School – Personal narratives
    I. Title   II. Hodgson, David
    792.8'07'10421   GV1788

    ISBN 0–423–00370–4

First published in Great Britain 1982
by Methuen Children's Books Ltd
11 New Fetter Lane, London EC4P 4EE
in association with Thames Television International Ltd
149 Tottenham Court Road, London W1P 9LL
Text copyright © 1982 David Hodgson
and Richard Glasstone
Illustrations copyright © 1982 Simon Rae-Scott
Printed in Great Britain by Fakenham Press, Norfolk

ISBN 0 423 00370 4

Introduction

What does it take to become a dancer? This depends on whether you are thinking of classical ballet, contemporary dance or showbusiness. But whatever style you choose, three things are essential; a strong, pliable body, a good sense of rhythmic co-ordination and the ability to work exceptionally hard.

Classical ballet is highly specialized. You need the right type of physique and to have started serious professional training by about the age of eleven – although a few dancers (mainly boys) do start a little later.

Most of the world's major ballet companies have their own schools. The School of American Ballet serves the New York City Ballet Company; the Paris Opera School is the oldest in the world; and the two most famous Russian schools are the Bolshoi and the Kirov. Britain's Royal Ballet School, which celebrated its fiftieth anniversary in 1981, is internationally recognized as one of the best.

Nearly all the dancers in the Royal Ballet are former pupils of the Royal Ballet School. Some come from other ballet schools, at the age of sixteen or seventeen, to join the Royal Ballet Upper School in West London; but most of the boys and many of the girls start their professional ballet training aged eleven or twelve, at White Lodge, the Royal Ballet Lower School.

Preliminary auditions for entry to White Lodge are held at regular intervals in a number of centres. Final auditions take place in London, ideally in the spring of the year before the candidate's eleventh birthday, although some children are accepted at twelve or – exceptionally – at thirteen years of age.

Very high standards are expected from every pupil and their progress and physical development are assessed every year. It is not always possible to predict exactly how a child's body is going to develop and sometimes the school has to advise a child not to continue as a classical dancer. Those who do continue to show sufficient promise and progress will graduate to the Upper School at the age of sixteen. After two to three years of further intensive training a number of them will join ballet companies either in Britain or abroad; but the main purpose of the School is to provide the corps de ballet, soloists and future stars of the Royal Ballet.

This book introduces four young dancers training at White Lodge; they hope one day to become part of the Royal Ballet Company. In their own words they tell us something about their training and their daily lives, about their ambitions and their dreams. We also see them featured in a series of specially created dances designed to express some of these feelings and experiences, as seen in the television film, *I Really Want to Dance*, on which this book is based.

Viviana Durante is thirteen and comes from Rome in Italy.

Viviana: 'I started ballet when I was eight years old, and I wanted to start because my best friend used to do it. Andre Prokovsky and Galina Samsova came to my old ballet school. They asked me if I wanted to try for the Royal Ballet School. So I said yes. I came over here from Italy to take an audition. I was a bit frightened because I didn't know what was happening. I couldn't say anything, I couldn't speak English.

Then, they wrote back to me saying that I had got through. I felt really happy because from when I was little I wanted to dance. I used to say to my mum, "Mum, can I go into a ballet school, can I go on the stage and do something? I really want to dance" '

Philip Mosley is twelve and comes from Cudworth, just outside Barnsley.

Philip: 'My big sister started dancing and I used to go and watch her. I nattered to my mum that I wanted to dance too and I started at the age of three. Before I came here I did festivals and competitions. In the last festival I got medals for tap, modern, ballet and Greek.

After that festival we got to know somebody who came here and she told my mum that I might get in. She gave my mum the address to write to and they sent us the audition forms.

We arrived in London and I was so excited. I'd never been on an underground train. When we got to the audition I didn't think I'd stand a chance, just seeing the other boys. The teachers were all smiling, trying to make you smile and be more confident. Well, after the final audition my mum and dad went up to the study and they told her that I had got through and when they came down my mum told me not to tell any of the others, just in case they hadn't.'

Anne Breckell is fourteen.
She comes from Maysmoor,
a little village near the city
of Gloucester.

Anne: 'I tried for the Royal Ballet School because my dancing teacher wanted me to, because another girl had already got in there and she wanted me to try.

I thought it would be very posh, red carpets and that. I didn't expect it to be so homely.

I thought it'd be stricter because my gran went to boarding school and she told me about what it was like then and I thought it'd still be like that.

I think the strictness here is just right really. I don't think there's any rules which do annoy me – we just like breaking them.'

Martin Corri is fifteen and
comes from Southend.

Martin: 'I was ten years old when I
started dancing. When I went to class I
felt rather embarrassed because I was the
only boy there, but after a while I got
used to it and just danced away.

I used to keep the secret from all the
boys at school apart from very good
friends. Some other boys found out in the
end and they used to tease me. They used
to say it was effeminate to be a dancer. I
thought they were wrong.

My teacher at home used to talk about
White Lodge and I thought that would
be very nice, so I just came around to
take an audition and got through.

At first my father thought it was a bit
cissy, but now he's come to terms with it
and he likes it quite a lot.

I like dancing with the music and in
the rhythm. When you're actually
dancing you seem to be hurting yourself,
but it's a very nice feeling. It's not really
hurting but physical endurance.
It's like an athlete because they're always
trained to run and even if it hurts, you
just keep on going and it's the same with
a dancer.'

White Lodge

White Lodge is situated in the middle of Richmond Park, Surrey. It was built by George I and was used by the British royal family for some two hundred years as an occasional residence. Since 1956 it has housed the younger pupils of the Royal Ballet School. Most of these 120 children are boarders, and more than a third are boys. As well as professional ballet training, they receive a good general education up to G.C.E. 'O' level. White Lodge is a Fee Assisted school and entry depends entirely on a child's physical suitability and natural talent for dancing.

Homesickness dance

In the dormitory, writing a letter to her parents, Viviana feels sad and homesick.

She is comforted by two of her friends, Sarah and Suzanne.

Philip: 'In the dormitory we play a lot of games and one of the games is called Ghost Train. We get all the beds and tip them upside down and make other people go through some tunnels. We pour water on their heads and put shampoo and toothpaste all over them.'

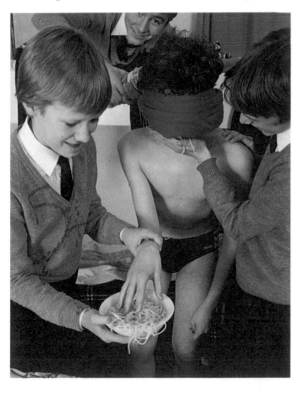

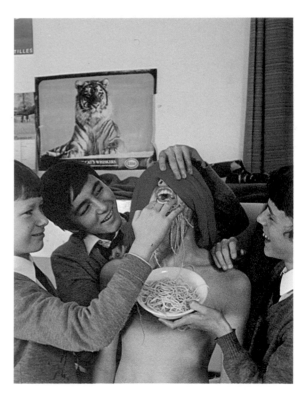

Education at White Lodge

The Royal Ballet School provides good, all–round education. The choice of subjects is of necessity more limited than in other, larger, schools, but there is some compensation in small classes and much individual attention.

Combining a professional training with full general education makes heavy demands on everyone concerned. At first, the dancing classes at White Lodge take up little more than one hour of the daily timetable; but this increases steadily as the pupils become more advanced. The growing balletic demands combined with the additional study needed for G.C.E. examinations mean that the pupils there have little free time compared with children of their age in ordinary schools.

Music is an important subject for dancers and most pupils at White Lodge learn to play an instrument. French is the modern language taught there because the first professional ballet academies were in France, and all the names of the dance steps are in French. The English department encourages the pupils' interest in Drama whilst Art is a subject that appeals to many of these children's sense of design.

It is always important for dancers to consider what work they might be suited to later on, when they are too old to dance; or indeed what they would turn to in the event of injury cutting short their ballet career. Even without that sort of misfortune, ballet dancing is a relatively short career, and most dancers retire from the stage by the time they reach middle age. A good, all round education is an invaluable asset when planning a second career.

Mathematics, History and Geography are some of the other subjects studied at White Lodge, as well as Human Biology, which dancers usually find interesting because it explains so much about how their own joints and muscles work.

Martin: 'Half of the day we do academic work and the other half we do ballet. I'm going to take two 'O' Levels – English Language and Art. I'm also taking Geography, French, English and Maths and I'm doing Biology C.S.E. Our Biology teacher is Mrs Keene. She's done quite a lot on the structure of the skeleton.'

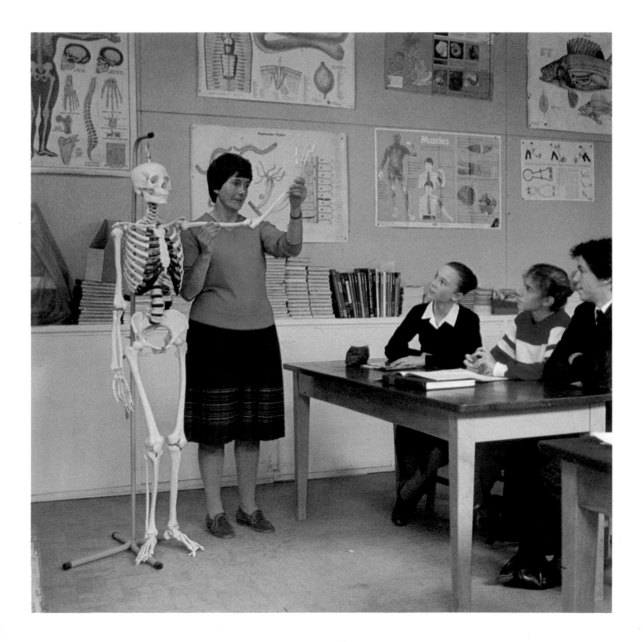

Skeleton dance

A daydream in a biology class. The boys
introduce Viviana to the skeleton who
invites her to dance with him. But her
dream becomes a nightmare and the boys
turn out to be the skeleton's henchmen.

A Ballet Class

A ballet class usually lasts one and a half hours. It always starts with the dancers at the 'barre', doing exercises to warm up and strengthen their muscles and make their bodies supple.

In the next part of class, known as centre practice, a number of the exercises are repeated without the support of the barre, and with more use of the arms and head.

Next comes 'adage', the slow movements that help dancers develop balance and poise; this is followed by pirouettes and other turns, small jumps, beaten steps and finally 'grand allegro', the sustained leaps.

This basic format is established right from the first year of serious training and remains an essential daily ritual throughout every dancer's career.

Anne: 'Our class starts at quarter to nine, so we are usually in the classroom by quarter past eight. We have to warm up different parts of the body to create warmer legs and knees, and things. We do back bends, forward bends and side bends to warm the waist and back.

The first part of class is spent at the barre. We do lots of exercises to warm up our muscles. We do the exercises over and over again, every day.'

Martin: 'The boys' ballet classes are completely separate from the girls' classes. We usually start the class at the barre – we do all those gruelling exercises you usually do like grands battements, ronds de jambe, tendus and pliés, at the barre. I think that's usually the hardest part of class.'

Anne: 'We practise things we're not too good at, like, say, pirouettes, because they can't be trusted. One day they could be really good and you feel really on balance and the next day they could just go, and you have to work extra hard to get what you had the day before. Some days you find it difficult because you push yourself too far so you fall off balance; some days your arms aren't working in co-ordination with your feet and you find it difficult.

I like doing pointe work. When you do pointe work you should feel very light, as if it's very easy, so the audience doesn't feel that it's a great load to get up on pointes.'

Martin: 'Half way through the class, after our legs are all warmed up and our bodies all hot and warm, we go into the centre but when you're in the centre you have to support yourself and use all your muscles.'

Martin: 'I like mainly very quick exercises, little allegro exercises and I like the jumps best.

At the end of class my shoulders ache and my feet hurt; I'm glad of the rest.'

Anne: 'Every girl must dream about doing Giselle and Swan Lake and Les Sylphides, because they're just part of ballet. I think we all must dream about being ballet dancers and being on stage – it's just natural.'

Rêverie

The music of this dance is called 'Rêverie'
– a dream. The choreography echoes
movements from Les Sylphides, a ballet
every girl dreams of dancing.

Assessments

One of the most difficult aspects of training at a professional school like White Lodge is having to face up to the possibility of failure. Helping the pupils to accept this and teaching them to look constructively at other alternatives to classical ballet dancing is an important part of their education.

Because such high standards are required in the dance profession, and because it is difficult to predict the exact pattern of a child's physical development, annual assessments are an integral part of a dancer's training.

If it becomes necessary to advise that a pupil should not continue at White Lodge, every effort is made to reach this decision within the first two years of training. This ensures that the pupil's education is not disturbed during the crucial years leading to C.S.E. and G.C.E examinations.

Each pupil's progress and physical development are carefully monitored during the five years they are at White Lodge and they are re-assessed at the end of the fifth year before being offered a place at the Upper School.

Viviana: 'The assessments are like a normal ballet class except that we are watched by the head of ballet and some other teachers. They look at you to see what progress you've made in the last year. If you don't get through these assessments you have to leave the school.

Assessments worry the children because everybody wants to get another year, but sometimes they can't and they get really upset about it. My best friend didn't get through this year and she's very sad about it because she doesn't want to leave the school.

You can fail assessments because sometimes you grow too tall or you cannot grow enough or you can become too fat or too thin. Or sometimes you're not developing sufficient dance quality. I think the assessments are necessary because then you can sort out who's going to be a dancer or not.'

Philip: 'Most of the children in the school
are learning a musical instrument. In the
timetable we are given time to practise
them. I'm learning the piano. During the
week I have five piano practices and two
music lessons.'

Piano dance

As Philip practises his five finger
exercises at the piano, the black and white
notes seem to come to life and he joins
them in a playful, abstract dance.

Strength training for boys

By the age of thirteen all boys at the Royal Ballet School are working regularly with weights to strengthen their arms, backs and legs. The emphasis is very much on accuracy and skill because this is in preparation for 'pas de deux' work – the art of partnering and lifting a ballerina.

The programme of strength training is carefully planned and graded. Before working with actual weights, the younger boys are taught the mechanics of each exercise in detail.

At the age of fourteen, after the boys have been working with weights for at least a year, they start classes in 'supported adage' which involves partnering girls but not yet lifting them. Lifting only begins in the final year at White Lodge, after two years of gradually intensified weight training. In this way boys are carefully prepared for the strenuous and complicated lifts they will be taught during the last phase of their training at the Upper School.

Pas de deux

Pas de deux classes are taken by Royal Ballet star David Drew.

Martin: 'Pas de deux means two people dancing together. I usually have Anne as my partner in pas de deux because she's about the right height – she's not too tall.'

Anne: 'Martin's very good but he's smaller than me, so sometimes I find it difficult to go under his arm. He has to go up on three quarter pointe so I can go under.

I do think it's essential that you like the person you're working with. If you're arguing a lot and you're always contradicting each other you don't enjoy it, and you have to enjoy pas de deux.'

Martin: 'When we start lifting the girls it seems quite a lot harder than lifting the weights because with the weights you just do exercises, just up and down, up and down; but with the girls you have to get the hands right, the feet right, the fingers in the right places, and it's a lot harder because the girls are also a lot heavier. You just have to keep them on balance.'

Anne: 'It's a nice feeling being lifted. Martin must be pretty strong because I weigh ... loads!'

Martin: 'Sometimes they think that they're doing all the work but they don't know what we're going through, trying to pick them up and turn them round.'

Martin is helped by choreographer Richard Glasstone.

Martin: 'At the end of the school year we put on a stage performance. Some of us are taught new dances and we have costumes fitted.'

'We also learn how to put on make-up. I don't like putting make-up on because it makes you look too much like a girl.

The thing I hate the most is lipstick because when you put your lips together you can't get them open again. They stick together – it's like glue.'

Anne: 'When I put on the make-up I feel the excitement coming for the performance and it's worth it, after all the rehearsals and things we've been doing.'

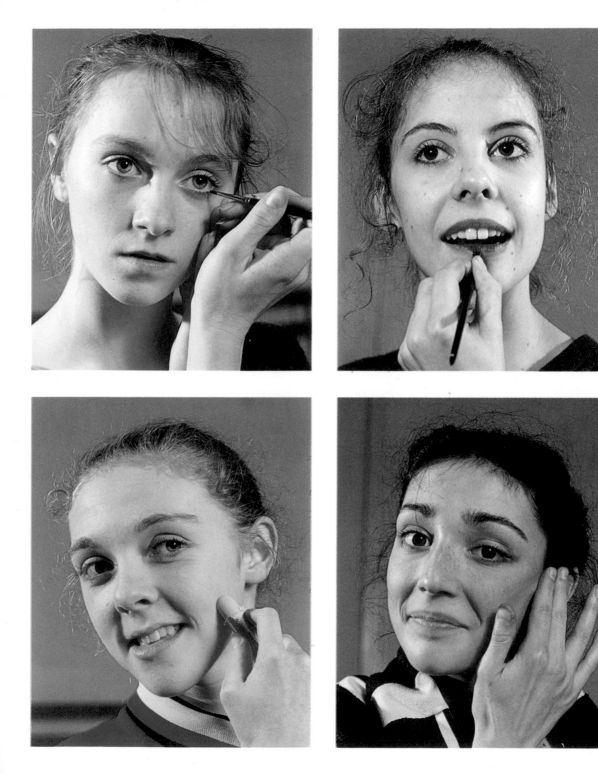

Danse Bohémienne

The pretty gypsy girl scorns her admirer, the sad, white-faced clown. She flirts with two other boys before rejecting them both for a handsome gypsy boy. There is a happy ending when the clown finds two other girls vying for his attention.

Philip: 'I hope to be a classical ballet dancer in the future. I like best of all ballet's flowingness.'

Anne: 'When you go on stage you really don't have the time to think "am I putting a foot right, or a foot wrong", you've just got to enjoy yourself and give the audience what you've got.'

Martin: 'As you grow older and get further up into the school it keeps growing within you and you just can't stop going, you just have to carry on and become part of what Anthony Dowell and David Wall have become.'

Viviana: 'I like being on stage and in contact with the audience. I hope to dance in the Royal Ballet company. I really want to dance.'

Richard Glasstone is the Senior Ballet Teacher for boys at White Lodge and Director of the Royal Ballet School's Dance Composition Course. After working internationally as a dancer, choreographer and teacher of ballet, he now specializes in choreography for young dancers. In addition to creating many ballets for the pupils of the Royal Ballet School, he has choreographed the film version of Benjamin Britten's *Friday Afternoons* presented by Thames Television under the title *Song and Dance*. He is the author of two other dance books, 'Better Ballet' and 'Male Dancing as a Career' both published by Kaye and Ward.

David Hodgson has been writing and producing documentaries for television for fifteen years. He has made many films about children and was awarded the Prix Jeunesse at Munich in 1972 and 1974. He has made three films featuring ballet: *Girl in a Broken Mirror*, *Song and Dance* and now, *I Really Want to Dance* which he devised as a 'documentary in dance'.

Simon Rae-Scott teaches English at the Royal Ballet School at White Lodge, where he has taken the opportunity to develop his interest in the highly demanding art of dance photography. This is the third book on which he has worked with Richard Glasstone and his photographs of the television production of *Song and Dance* were featured widely in the ballet press.

Dancers

Loreen Flowerdew	Susanne Thomas
Sara Gallie	Adam Horton
Katharine Harbottle	Gary Lambert
Meryl Holloway	David Newson
Linda Keens	Kevin O'Hare
Alice Komlosy	Jeremy Sheffield
Simonetta Lysy	James Taylor
Sarah McKeating	Brent Williamson

Costume designer: Heather Magoon
Ballet Mistress: Pauline Wadsworth

Film Production Team
Lighting cameraman: Raymond Sieman
Sound recordist: Brian Rendle
Film Editor: Rosemary Macloughlin
Production Assistant: Christine Hill